Gypsum Public Library
P.O. Box 979 / 47 Lundgren Blvd.
Gypsum, CO 81637
(970) 524-5080

THE UNTOLD HISTORY
OF ANCIENT CIVILIZATIONS

GREEKS

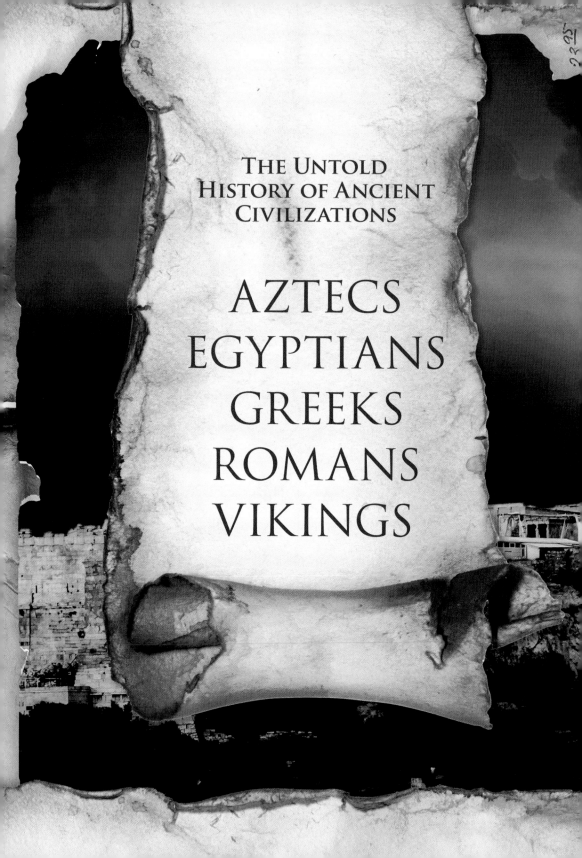

THE UNTOLD
HISTORY OF ANCIENT
CIVILIZATIONS

AZTECS
EGYPTIANS
GREEKS
ROMANS
VIKINGS

THE UNTOLD HISTORY
OF ANCIENT CIVILIZATIONS

GREEKS

MASON CREST
PHILADELPHIA
MIAMI

Mason Crest
450 Parkway Drive, Suite D
Broomall, Pennsylvania 19008
(866) MCP-BOOK (toll-free)
www.masoncrest.com

Copyright © 2019 by Mason Crest, an imprint of National Highlights, Inc. All rights reserved. No part of this publication may be reproduced or transmitted in any form or by any means, electronic or mechanical, including photocopying, recording, taping, or any information storage and retrieval system, without permission from the publisher.
First printing
9 8 7 6 5 4 3 2 1

ISBN (hardback) 978-1-4222-3520-1
ISBN (series) 978-1-4222-3517-1
ISBN (ebook 978-1-4222-8340-0

Cataloging-in-Publication Data on file with the Library of Congress

Developed and produced by Mason Crest
Editor: Keri De Deo
Interior and cover design: Jana Rade
Production: Michelle Luke

QR CODES AND LINKS TO THIRD-PARTY CONTENT
You may gain access to certain third-party content ("Third-Party Sites") by scanning and using the QR Codes that appear in this publication (the "QR Codes"). We do not operate or control in any respect  any information, products, or services on such Third-Party Sites linked to by us via the QR Codes included in this publication, and we assume no responsibility for any materials you may access using the QR Codes. Your use of the QR Codes may be subject to terms, limitations, or restrictions set forth in the applicable terms of use or otherwise established by the owners of the Third-Party Sites. Our linking to such Third-Party Sites via the QR Codes does not imply an endorsement or sponsorship of such Third-Party Sites or the information, products, or services offered on or through the Third-Party Sites, nor does it imply an endorsement or sponsorship of this publication by the owners of such Third-Party Sites.

CONTENTS

KEY ICONS TO LOOK FOR:

WORDS TO UNDERSTAND: These words with their easy-to-understand definitions will increase the reader's understanding of the text while building vocabulary skills.

SIDEBARS: This boxed material within the main text allows readers to build knowledge, gain insights, explore possibilities, and broaden their perspectives by weaving together additional information to provide realistic and holistic perspectives.

EDUCATIONAL VIDEOS: Readers can view videos by scanning our QR codes, providing them with additional educational content to supplement the text. Examples include news coverage, moments in history, speeches, iconic sports moments, and much more!

TEXT-DEPENDENT QUESTIONS: These questions send the reader back to the text for more careful attention to the evidence presented there.

RESEARCH PROJECTS: Readers are pointed toward areas of further inquiry connected to each chapter. Suggestions are provided for projects that encourage deeper research and analysis.

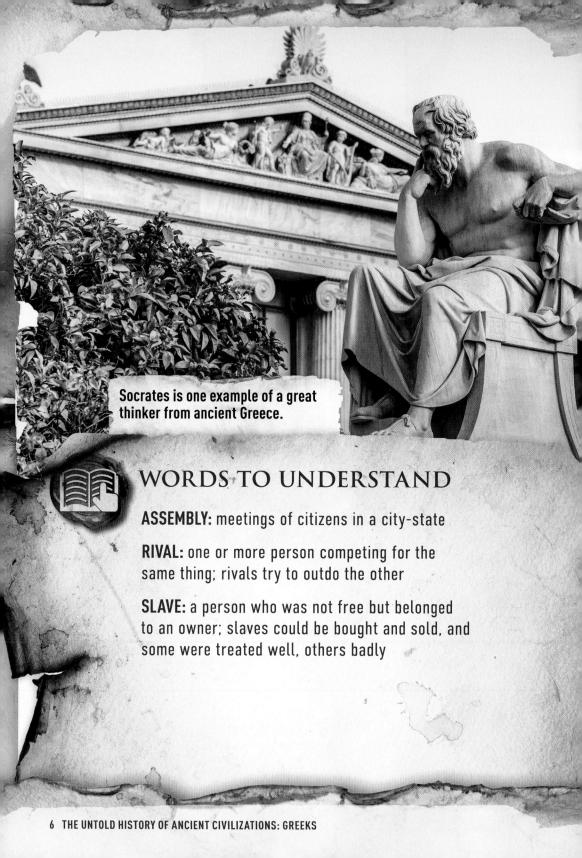

Socrates is one example of a great thinker from ancient Greece.

WORDS TO UNDERSTAND

ASSEMBLY: meetings of citizens in a city-state

RIVAL: one or more person competing for the same thing; rivals try to outdo the other

SLAVE: a person who was not free but belonged to an owner; slaves could be bought and sold, and some were treated well, others badly

CHAPTER 1

A PEEK AT THE GREEKS

The Greeks were on top of the European world from around 600 to 200 BC. Western society owes a lot to them.

The Greeks had pride in their cities, soldiers, arts and crafts, poems and plays, thinkers, scientists, and politicians. They pitied people who were not Greeks and felt that everyone else was uncivilized.

Greece was divided into many city-states, which were cities with farms and countryside around them. All city-states were fierce **rivals**, and their citizens loved to call each other names. Athenians were smug and bossy, Spartans were cheats and liars, Corinthians were soft, and Thebans were traitors, which was the worst insult of all. The biggest rivalry was probably between Athens, the strongest naval power, and the Spartans, the strongest land power.

JUPITER
ROMAN

ZEUS
GREEK

Watch this video for a brief history of ancient Greece.

Aα Bβ Γγ Δδ Εε Ζζ
Ηη Θθ Ιι Κκ Λλ Μμ
Νν Ξξ Οο Ππ Ρρ Σσς
Ττ Υυ Φφ Χχ Ψψ Ωω

Many English letters and words come from the Greek language.

Each city-state had its own laws. Some of these were very old. Citizens claimed that they had been made by gods or by mythical leaders, like Solon and Lycurgus, who probably never existed. (This is not as strange as it sounds; it was a way of saying that the old laws deserved respect.) New laws were made by an **assembly** and approved by a senate, like in democracies (government by the people) today. Scientists say democracy was invented in Athens around 500 BC. However, only male citizens over thirty could take part. Women, foreigners, young men, and **slaves** were banned.

GREEK SPEAK

The ancient Greeks thought their language was the best in the world. They called foreigners "barbarians" because their words sounded like silly sheep bleating: "baa, baa, baa."

Hello/goodbye: *khaire* (say "khy-re")
Please: *ei soi dokei* (say "ay soy dok-ay")
Thank you: *kharin oida soi* (say "khar-in oy-da soy")
Yes: *nai* (say "ny")
No: *oukhi* (say "ook-hi")
Where?: *pou* (say "poo")
When?: *pote* (say "po-tay")
Help!: *boethei* (say "bo-air-thay")

This map shows the extent of ancient Greece at the height of its rule.

This clock in Rome, Italy, is powered purely by water.

TEXT-DEPENDENT QUESTIONS

1. When were the Greeks at the top of European power?
2. Name three of the city-states of Greece.
3. How were new laws made?

RESEARCH PROJECT

MAKE A WATER CLOCK

The ancient Greeks did not have clocks with springs, batteries, or electricity. They used water clocks, called clepsydra, instead. (These went drip-drop instead of tick-tock!) Here is how to make one. It might be best to try this outside because it could be messy.

YOU WILL NEED:

- Two plastic containers both about the same size (You could use big yogurt containers or the bottom halves of two soft drinks bottles.)
- A bendy drinking straw
- Scissors
- Plastic bricks or a plastic box
- A small piece of plastic food wrap
- A small rubber band
- Water

INSTRUCTIONS:

1. Using scissors, carefully make a small hole in one of the containers, near the bottom. It should be just big enough for the straw to fit in.

2. Trim the straw, so it looks like the straw in the diagram.

3. Push one end of the straw into the hole. Cover the other end of the straw with food wrap. Use the elastic band to hold the wrap in place.

4. Stand the container on the bricks or box. Put the other container below it.

5. Fill the top container with water, and carefully remove the food wrap and elastic band.

6. See how long the water takes to run out into the lower container. It will be the same every time.

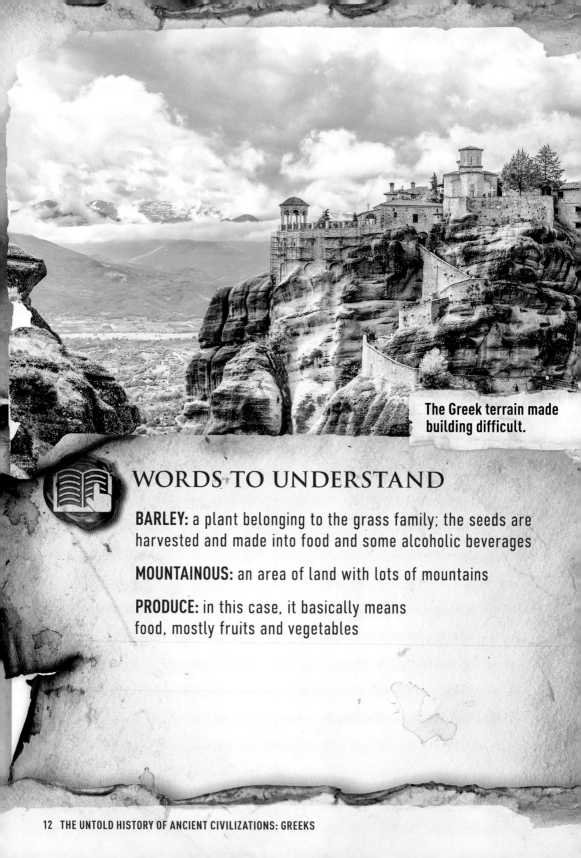

The Greek terrain made building difficult.

WORDS TO UNDERSTAND

BARLEY: a plant belonging to the grass family; the seeds are harvested and made into food and some alcoholic beverages

MOUNTAINOUS: an area of land with lots of mountains

PRODUCE: in this case, it basically means food, mostly fruits and vegetables

CHAPTER 2

TAMING THE WILDS

It was not easy living in Greece. The landscape was wild and **mountainous,** and the climate was harsh, with scorching summers and stormy winters. It was difficult to grow food to support the population, and it was hard to get around. It was often easier to go by sea, though shipwrecks were common. So were pirate attacks. Worst of all, Greece lay in a violent earthquake zone.

You can see the ancient terraces on this Greek mountainside in Peloponnese.

The olive harvest was important to the survival of Greeks.

But the Greeks were great survivors. Most people lived in the country and worked on farms. Only about 20 percent of the land in the country could grow crops. Greek farmers built terraces, like steps in steep, rocky hillsides, and dug ditches to carry water from mountain streams.

Farmers' main crops were **barley**, grapes, and olives. They also grew onions, lettuce, and garlic. Pigs, scraggy sheep, and goats could be found on some

A CASE OF TREE ABUSE?

Each year, farmers gathered ripe olives by beating the trees until the fruit fell down. Then they crushed the olives between stones to get oil. They ate olive oil raw in food and used it for cooking, as a skin cleanser and hair conditioner, and as a medicine. Other ways to use it included softening leather and burning in lamps. Olive oil was so valued that it was also a prize in sports competitions and an offering to the gods.

farms. The Greeks went hunting for hares, deer, and even hedgehogs, if no other meat could be found. Wives and children gathered mushrooms, wild fruit, and nuts in the forests, hoping not to meet wild boars or bears.

Without freezers or refrigerators, it was not easy to make **produce** last through the winter. Cheese was wrapped in leaves or floated in jars of oil. Barley was ground between stones, mixed with oil, seeds, and spices, and then covered with bran and stored in wooden tubs. (Weeks later, this sticky paste was eaten raw. Even the Greeks did not really like it, but it was better than nothing.)

The ancient Greeks stored cheese in oil to help preserve it.

TEXT-DEPENDENT QUESTIONS

1. How did the ancient Greeks survive such a harsh landscape?
2. How did farmers harvest ripe olives?
3. Without freezers or refrigerators, how did the Greeks make their food last?

RESEARCH PROJECT

Like the Greeks, other ancient civilizations didn't have refrigerators or freezers. How did other civilizations keep their food from spoiling? Do some research and create a three- to five-page report explaining how different ancient civilizations kept their food fresh.

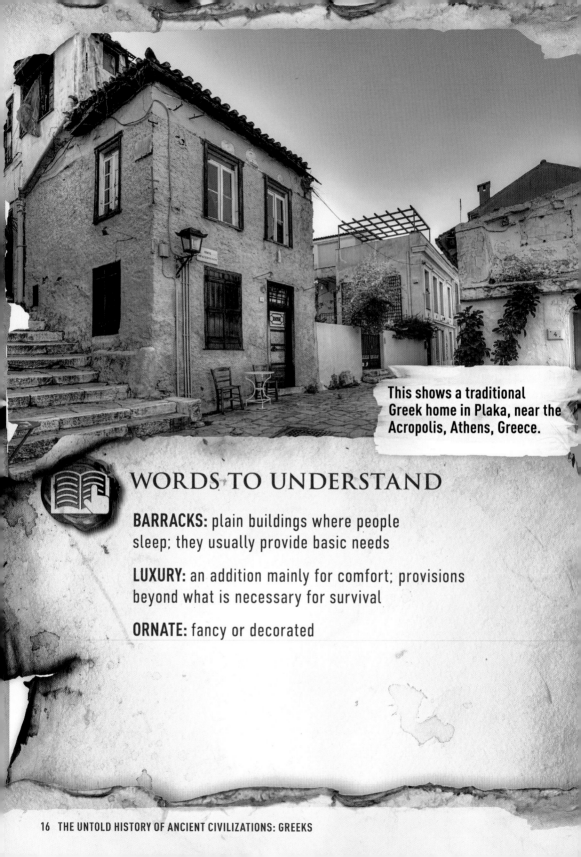

This shows a traditional Greek home in Plaka, near the Acropolis, Athens, Greece.

WORDS TO UNDERSTAND

BARRACKS: plain buildings where people sleep; they usually provide basic needs

LUXURY: an addition mainly for comfort; provisions beyond what is necessary for survival

ORNATE: fancy or decorated

CHAPTER 3

HOME GREEK HOME

Greek houses were different in different city-states. In most of Greece, ordinary homes began with just a living room and a bedroom, but over the years, homeowners added more rooms. These rooms were built around a private courtyard. But in Sparta, for example, men lived in **barracks** and only visited their wives at home.

Rich families also built new rooms to display their wealth. They added **luxuries**, such as running water from diverted streams. But, because there were no drains, they still used buckets for bathrooms like everyone else. They hung woven rugs on the walls and bought carved wooden furniture, including couches, chests, chairs, and low tables. But the styles were kept simple. The most **ornate** furniture was placed in public buildings.

BE HOME BY DARK

At night, Greek city streets could be dangerous. You might meet prowling robbers, muggers and hooligans, drunken partygoers, or even enemy spies. Or you might trip over people sleeping in doorways or slip and fall on the rough ground. People who needed to go out at night took an escort of slaves with flaming torches and big sticks.

Greek families worried about security. Because walls were made of mud and brick, determined robbers, known as "wall diggers," could break in. There was only one door into a house, and it was guarded by a slave or a dog. Privacy was also important. Most houses had a room for women only that men could not enter. They had a separate room of their own for entertaining male friends.

Houses could sometimes seem like prisons. Women, children, and slaves all needed a man's permission to leave. Slaves and women from poor families were allowed out to fetch water or buy food. But rich women, from "respectable" families, could leave only to take part in religious ceremonies and funerals or to visit other women. In Sparta, however, women had more freedom. They could move through public alone, participate in sporting events, and even own land!

The Greek style is known for its simplicity.

TEXT-DEPENDENT QUESTIONS

1. Describe the housing in Sparta. How was this different from other city-states?
2. How was housing different in rich homes than in poor homes?
3. Why were robbers known as "wall diggers"?

RESEARCH PROJECT

Not all Greeks had running water in their homes. When did running water become a standard feature in most homes across the world? Are there still places where people do not have indoor running water? What are these places, and how do they get water? Do some research, and prepare a visual presentation about your findings using poster board or a computer program. Ask your teacher if you can present this in class.

Hera, the wife of Zeus, is the Olympian goddess of marriage, protector of family and married women.

WORDS TO UNDERSTAND

CLAN: people descended from one ancestor; they had a duty to help one another

DEFORMED: something that does not look average; misshapen

HEARTH: the center of a house or village where a fire was lit and where most activity took place

CHAPTER 4

FAMILY TIES

The Greeks did not have a word for "family." You belonged to a **clan** and a household. Your clan meant your blood relations, people descended from a common ancestor. Your household was the people you lived with—your mom and dad, brothers and sisters, grandparents, servants, and slaves.

Greek marriages were often arranged. Women had no say in who their husbands would be. Husbands and wives might not even see each other before their wedding day. Once married, they were not equal. Husbands had almost total power over money and legal matters, though wives were in charge of running the home.

When a Greek baby was born, the father had a big decision to make. He might not want another baby boy because the family land would have to be split when he died. And it cost money to have a daughter marry. Weak or **deformed** babies, too, were often abandoned or given to childless couples.

This video explains how women were viewed in different city-states in ancient Greece.

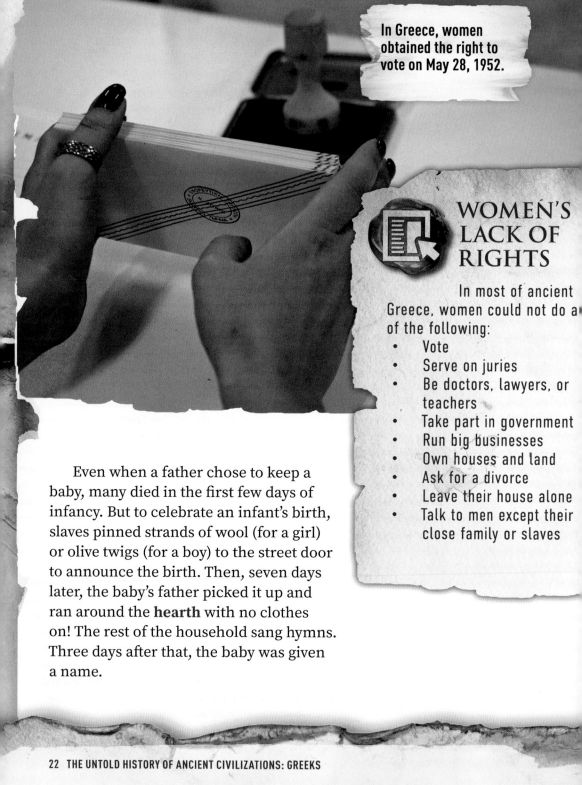

In Greece, women obtained the right to vote on May 28, 1952.

WOMEN'S LACK OF RIGHTS

In most of ancient Greece, women could not do a of the following:

- Vote
- Serve on juries
- Be doctors, lawyers, or teachers
- Take part in government
- Run big businesses
- Own houses and land
- Ask for a divorce
- Leave their house alone
- Talk to men except their close family or slaves

Even when a father chose to keep a baby, many died in the first few days of infancy. But to celebrate an infant's birth, slaves pinned strands of wool (for a girl) or olive twigs (for a boy) to the street door to announce the birth. Then, seven days later, the baby's father picked it up and ran around the **hearth** with no clothes on! The rest of the household sang hymns. Three days after that, the baby was given a name.

The ancient Greeks
valued the family unit.

In ancient Greece, fathers named their babies when they were about ten days old.

This statue of Alexander the Great can be found in Thessaloniki City in Greece.

TEXT-DEPENDENT QUESTIONS

1. How did the Greeks define "family"?
2. What rights did women not have?
3. What did fathers do to celebrate the birth of a child?

RESEARCH PROJECT

ENJOY SOME ANCIENT GREEK STORIES

Many stories told by Greek "song-stitchers" are still popular today. You can find them in your school or public library. Look for books telling the strange adventures of the Greek hero Odysseus and all the magical monsters he met. Or read about brave Greek soldiers and how they conquered their enemies at Troy with a very clever trick. Using one of the stories as your guide, write your own story similar to a Greek adventure.

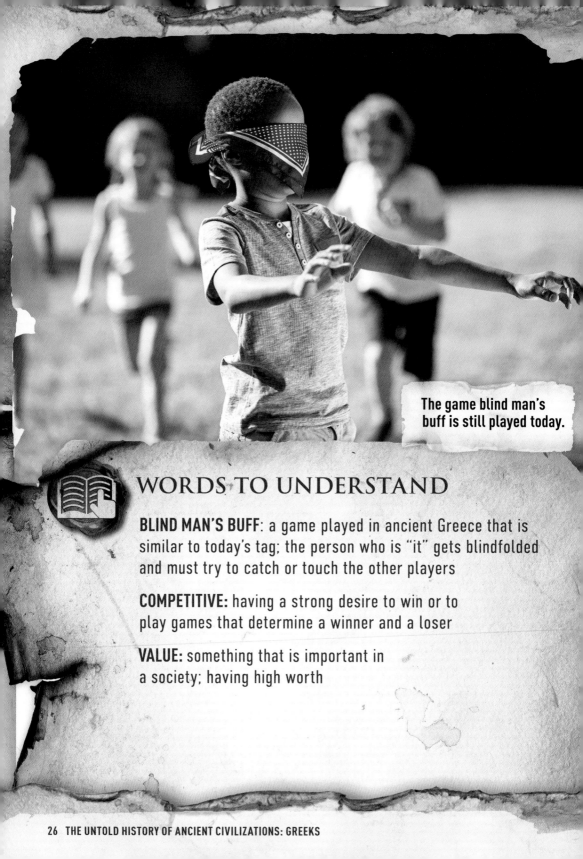

The game blind man's buff is still played today.

WORDS TO UNDERSTAND

BLIND MAN'S BUFF: a game played in ancient Greece that is similar to today's tag; the person who is "it" gets blindfolded and must try to catch or touch the other players

COMPETITIVE: having a strong desire to win or to play games that determine a winner and a loser

VALUE: something that is important in a society; having high worth

CHAPTER 5

WINNER TAKE ALL

G reek children loved to play, and many of their games and toys were like ours today. They had dolls, rattles, yo-yos, dice, spinning tops, seesaws, and puppets. They played hockey, tug-of-war, and **blind man's buff** (later called "blind man's bluff"). But some of their games were rather different. One favorite was played with the anklebones of dead sheep. All games were very **competitive**, and to win, kids were encouraged to use tricks if they had to.

TOUGH LOVE

In Sparta, a Greek city-state, boys' lives were very hard. At age seven, they were taken away from their families to live in army camps. They were kept cold and hungry, and baths were banned. They were often beaten. If they died, it proved they were too weak to survive. Spartan girls stayed at home but learned tough sports and fighting like boys. Self-denial and simplicity were the most important values Spartans taught their children.

Teenagers were kept busy, so they would not misbehave. Girls were married at twelve or fourteen. Teenage boys worked or went to school. Often, they went to sports centers to get healthy exercise. At eighteen, they had to join the army for two years.

This little toy horse, on display at the Museum of the Ancient Agora in Athens, Greece, dates back to 900 BC.

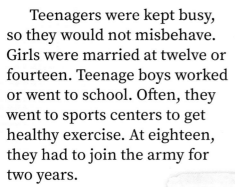

This image memorializes the Spartan soldiers in Thermopylae, Greece.

Sparta is well known for its warriors. This statue is in the central square of Sparta, Greece.

The spinning top is
a game traced back
to ancient Greece.

TEXT-DEPENDENT QUESTIONS

1. What are some of the games the Greeks played?
2. What happened when boys turned seven in Sparta?
3. Why were teenagers kept so busy?

RESEARCH PROJECT

HOW TO MAKE A SPINNING TOP

YOU WILL NEED:

- A plastic lid
- Blank piece of paper slightly bigger than the plastic lid (make sure it's one that no one wants back)
- A pencil
- Scissors
- A marshmallow stick (or wooden skewer)
- Glue
- Sequins, or some other decorations

INSTRUCTIONS:

1. Find a plastic lid, and trace it onto a blank piece of paper.
2. Cut out the circle.
3. Fold the circle in half twice.
4. Grab the paper, and place it in the center of the lid.
5. Poke a hole (not too hard) in the middle of the paper so it will go through the lid.
6. Glue the paper to the plastic lid.
7. Take a marshmallow stick (or wooden skewer) and pull it through the hole with the paper side up, being careful not to poke your finger.
8. Take the lid off, and decorate it (on the paper). You can make a spiral with the glue and put sequins on top, or use other craft materials and make your own design.
9. Put the stick back in.
10. Spin the top once it is almost or already dry. Some decorations may shoot off as it is spinning, so then you will know what to glue back on more securely!

Adapted from WikiHow.com

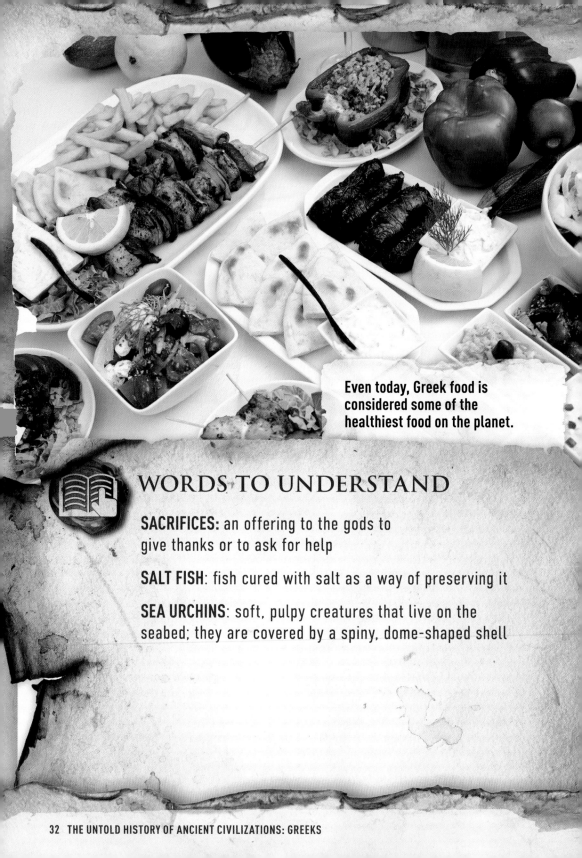

Even today, Greek food is considered some of the healthiest food on the planet.

WORDS TO UNDERSTAND

SACRIFICES: an offering to the gods to give thanks or to ask for help

SALT FISH: fish cured with salt as a way of preserving it

SEA URCHINS: soft, pulpy creatures that live on the seabed; they are covered by a spiny, dome-shaped shell

CHAPTER 6

BORING BUT HEALTHY

Greek food was plain and simple—no fancy sauces or hot spices, a fact that visitors to Greece at the time complained about in their writings. The ancient Greeks cooked most of their food. A typical meal might be bread, **salt fish**, fruit or vegetables, and olive oil. The usual drink, even at breakfast time, was wine mixed with water.

Salted, dried fish was a staple in the ancient Greek diet.

Meat was an expensive luxury. Many families looked forward to religious festival days because that was their only chance to eat it. Priests roasted animals that had been **sacrificed** to the gods over fires in front of temples and handed out slices of meat to worshippers. The Greeks also shared another favorite food—barley cakes sweetened with honey—with their gods. Sugar was unknown in ancient Greek times. They had a very healthy diet.

I'LL HAVE THE OCTOPUS

The ancient Greeks ate foods that some people might not like today, such as goats' lungs (the air inside whistled as they were cooked), **sea urchins** (raw and still alive), and octopus (very tough and chewy). But for them, food was often a matter of survival, not choice. When food was scarce, in wartime or drought years, Greeks ate almost anything they could find, including iris roots, beechnuts, lupin seeds, and grasshoppers.

Sea urchin is considered a delicacy in many cultures.

The Greeks liked cheese but made it from sheep's milk, not cow's. They thought cow's milk was unhealthy. They also enjoyed soups made with lentils and chickpeas.

Meat may have been scarce, but many Greeks chose to be vegetarians. Led by the philosopher Pythagoras, they believed that all animals had souls. Strangely, he felt beans contained the same materials, and he forbade his followers from eating them too.

Normally, Greeks ate sitting on low chairs. But on special occasions, such as men-only dinner parties, they ate lying down. Diners relaxed on long, low couches, which had room for two, side by side. This was so comfortable that they often dozed off between courses. Or maybe the wine was to blame?

This ancient Greek bowl, dated to the fifth or sixth century was probably used for wine.

TEXT-DEPENDENT QUESTIONS

1. Why did visitors to Greece complain about the food?
2. What kind of food did the ancient Greeks sacrifice to the gods?
3. Where did the Greeks eat?

RESEARCH PROJECT

To some people, the food ancient Greeks ate may seem strange. What other "strange" foods do other cultures eat? Do an Internet search for some interesting or bizarre food choices, and create a short presentation on the varieties of food people eat to survive. Consider some of the food you eat. Would other cultures find the food you eat odd to them?

We know a lot about ancient Greek clothing from the sculptures and artwork left behind.

WORDS TO UNDERSTAND

LOINCLOTH: a strip of cloth wound round the lower body

PHILOSOPHER: a highly educated person; philosophers were often in charge of respected places of learning

SCHOLAR: a person who knows a lot about one subject

CHAPTER 7

LOOKING THE PART

Clothes for Greek men, women, and children were all made from a single piece of cloth wrapped around the body and held in place by pins. From paintings, scientists can tell that they were very colorful with intricate designs. Underneath, some men wore a **loincloth**, and some women covered their chests with a soft cloth band. But most Greeks wore no underwear at all!

It was up to the women in the home to make all the cloth for the clothes their families wore. Clothes for men and children were usually knee-length. Women's clothes reached the floor, and so did robes for priests and kings.

A sign of being rich was to wear fancy cloth woven from Chinese silk and dyed purple with "murex" (rotted shellfish). It could be bought at markets for a high price. But some **scholars** turned their backs on such shows of wealth. They deliberately wore

This school project by Madeline Webb demonstrates the different clothing styles for men and women of ancient Greece.

old, shabby clothes as a sign that they were thinking of more important things. One famous **philosopher**, Diogenes (about 400–325 BC), gave up clothes altogether and lived in a big pottery jar.

Greek women, that is, rich Greek women, used makeup, hair dye, and perfume. Their idea of beauty was to have pale skin and light hair. They let their hair grow long and tied it back with ribbons or jeweled headbands. Men had short hair and neatly trimmed beards. Slaves had their hair cut very short to show they were not free.

Many of the ancient Greek measurements were based on the size of an average man.

THE MEASURE OF A MAN

The ancient Greeks measured length and distance in units based on an average-sized adult man.

1 finger = almost 1 inch (2.5 cm)
4 fingers = 1 palm = 3 inches (7.5 cm)
12 fingers = 1 hand-span = 9 inches (22.5 cm)
16 fingers = 1 foot (30 cm)
24 fingers = 1 cubit = 18 inches (46 cm)
1 pace = 2.5 feet (75 cm)
1 stretch (both arms) = 6 feet (1.8m)
1 stadion = 600 feet (178m)

TEXT-DEPENDENT QUESTIONS

1. How do scientists know what the Greeks wore?
2. In Greek measurements, what body part equals 1 inch (2.5 cm)?
3. What kind of clothing was a sign of being rich?

RESEARCH PROJECT

MAKE YOUR OWN GREEK CLOTHING

Ancient Greeks wore one or two pieces of cloth wrapped around their body. You can learn how to make one by following these directions:

You will need:

- White flat bed sheet
- Piece of string or a belt
- Safety pins

Directions for a basic dress:

1. Take a corner of the sheet in one hand, leaving about 6 to 8 inches to spare. Hold the sheet in front of the top of your right shoulder.
2. Drape the sheet across your chest, and tuck it under your left arm.
3. Wrap the sheet around your back. Tuck it under your right arm and once more around the front of your chest.
4. After bringing the sheet across your chest, under your left arm the second time and around your back, bring the second corner up over your back. Secure the two ends with a knot.
5. Secure the layers tightly with a couple of hidden safety pins inside the toga.
6. Add a belt around your waist.
7. Combine the dress with sandals, and you'll have an authentic-looking Greek costume.

There are many styles of clothing. Do an Internet search for videos demonstrating different styles to try.

Adapted from hercampus.com

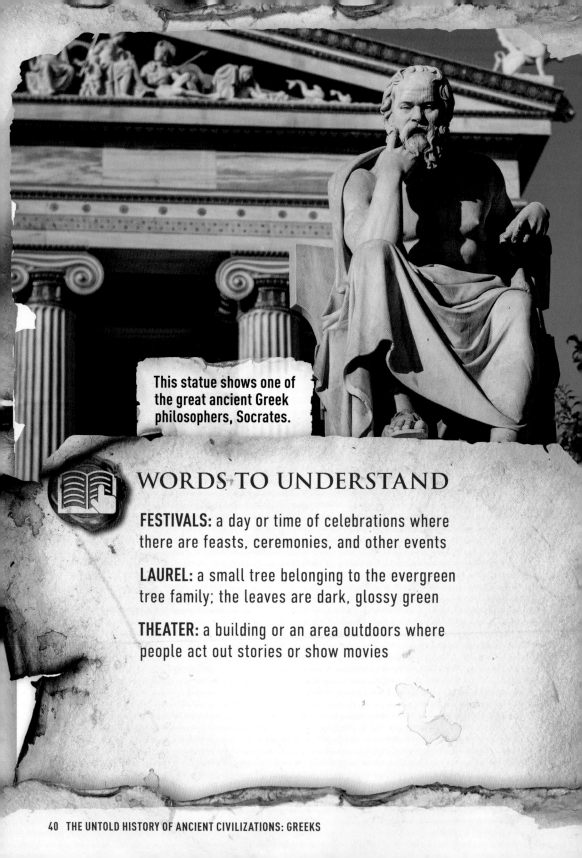

This statue shows one of the great ancient Greek philosophers, Socrates.

WORDS TO UNDERSTAND

FESTIVALS: a day or time of celebrations where there are feasts, ceremonies, and other events

LAUREL: a small tree belonging to the evergreen tree family; the leaves are dark, glossy green

THEATER: a building or an area outdoors where people act out stories or show movies

CHAPTER 8

SERIOUS FUN

The Greeks tried to live their lives to the fullest. They loved to discuss important questions, such as "When did the world begin?" They attracted the world's best scientists and cleverest thinkers to their city-states with big pay. Socrates, Plato, and Aristotle are probably the best-known Greek philosophers today. But they also enjoyed parties, singing, dancing, going to the **theater**, telling stories, laughing at jokes, and playing games.

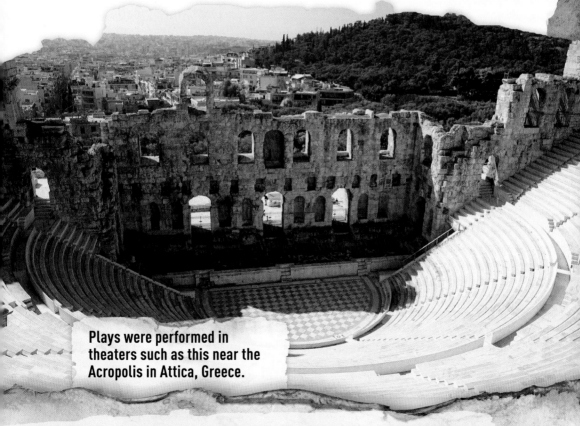

Plays were performed in theaters such as this near the Acropolis in Attica, Greece.

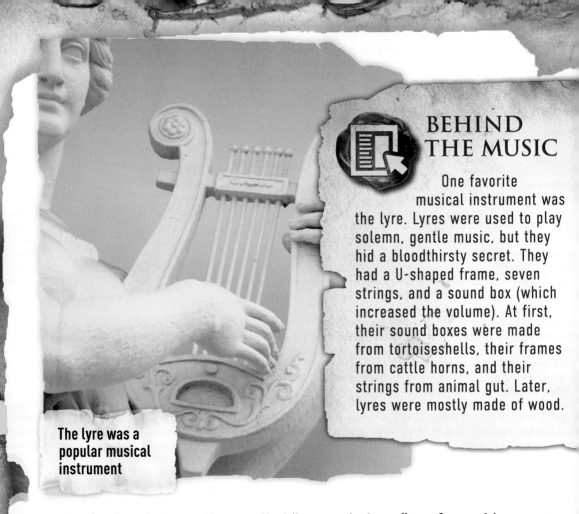

BEHIND THE MUSIC

BEHIND THE MUSIC

One favorite musical instrument was the lyre. Lyres were used to play solemn, gentle music, but they hid a bloodthirsty secret. They had a U-shaped frame, seven strings, and a sound box (which increased the volume). At first, their sound boxes were made from tortoiseshells, their frames from cattle horns, and their strings from animal gut. Later, lyres were mostly made of wood.

The lyre was a popular musical instrument

Professional storytellers, called "song-stitchers," performed in streets and markets and at **festivals**. They told the stories of the gods but added their own touches. Guests at dinner parties also told jokes and stories and played silly games like kottabos, which involved flicking drops of wine at a target.

The Greeks liked music and dancing because they were fun. They were also part of many religious ceremonies. Sometimes, worshippers got carried away by the beat. Stories were told of maenads, wild women who left their homes and ran to the mountains, where they tore wild beasts limb from limb. They followed the god of wine, Dionysus.

Sport was the most important entertainment of all. The famous Olympic Games, held in honor of the god Zeus, was just one of many sports festivals open to all Greek athletes. Like football and baseball today, they inspired fierce rivalry and local pride. Champions were sponsored by rich businessmen and were rewarded with free food for life by their home city. Winning athletes wore crowns of **laurel** leaves, pine branches, or wild celery. Milon of Croton was one of the early famous Olympic champions. He won men's wrestling five times.

The original Olympic games were held at Olympia.

TEXT-DEPENDENT QUESTIONS

1. Who are some of the best-known Greek philosophers?
2. What was a favorite musical instrument?
3. Why were the first Olympic Games held?

RESEARCH PROJECT

HOLD YOUR OWN OLYMPIC GAMES

To celebrate the Olympics, you can create your own games and make your own medals. Have races with your friends, design your own team flag, play frisbee, use brooms to create your own curling or hockey game . . . the ideas are endless! Hold a ceremony to celebrate the players and participants.

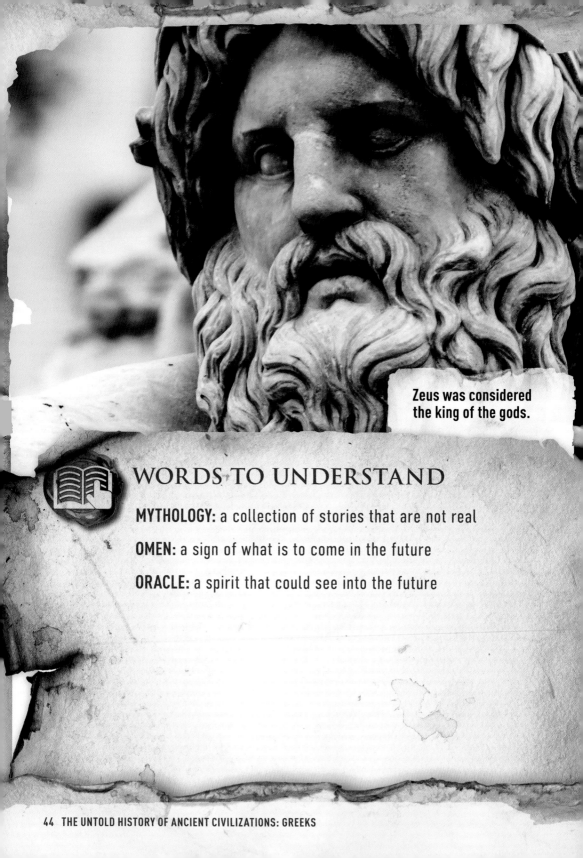

Zeus was considered
the king of the gods.

WORDS TO UNDERSTAND

MYTHOLOGY: a collection of stories that are not real

OMEN: a sign of what is to come in the future

ORACLE: a spirit that could see into the future

CHAPTER 9

SUPERHUMAN, BUT NOT ALWAYS HEROES

G reek gods and goddesses were bigger than life. They were taller, stronger, and more beautiful than any human. But they were also greedier, trickier, and more vengeful. They had magic powers and lived forever. Many gods helped their favorite people or cities, whereas others used them to get back at their enemies.

The Parthenon as built as a temple for the ancient Greek gods.

To keep the gods happy, the Greeks gave them presents, called sacrifices. Human sacrifice is often described in Greek **mythology**, but scientists are still not sure whether the Greeks actually did it. Most often, the Greeks gave animals, food, or wine.

The Greeks built huge temples, but they didn't go inside. A temple was a god's house and too holy, except for priests and priestesses. Some that you can still see today are the Parthenon and the Temple of Hephaestus.

A few mythical gods and goddesses were worshipped secretly, in the wild countryside or in hidden caves. Some special underground rituals to honor Demeter, goddess of fertility, were so mysterious that no one knows what went on, even today. Anyone who tried to tell was killed instantly.

The goddess, Demeter, was considered a fertility god.

ALL IN THE MYTHICAL FAMILY

This "family" of gods and goddesses lived on Olympus, the highest mountain in Greece.

Aphrodite—goddess of love and beauty
Apollo—god of music and learning
Ares—god of war
Artemis—goddess of young girls and wild creatures
Athena—goddess of wisdom, arts and crafts, and war
Demeter—goddess of grain and growing crops
Dionysus—god of wine and wildness
Hera—goddess of women and marriage
Hermes—messenger of the gods
Hestia—goddess of hearths and homes
Poseidon—god of earthquakes and the sea
Zeus—god of lightning, king of the gods

Spirits living in fields, streams, and trees were also worshipped by the Greeks. They believed that some spirits, called **oracles**, could see into the future and understand the will of the gods. Priests talked to oracle trees and hung prayers in their branches. They also examined the guts of dead animals for **omens**. At Delphi, the most well-known oracle, a priestess, drugged with smoke from burning leaves, gave answers to questions.

This is the stone monument known as the Omphalos of Delphi.

TEXT-DEPENDENT QUESTIONS

1. What did the ancient Greeks do to keep the gods and goddesses happy?
2. Where did the gods and goddesses live?
3. What talents did some of the spirits possess?

RESEARCH PROJECT

Research some of the ancient Greek gods. What did they look like? What did they do? What happened to them? How are some of these mythical creatures thought of today? Create a visual presentation, or write a paper about your findings.

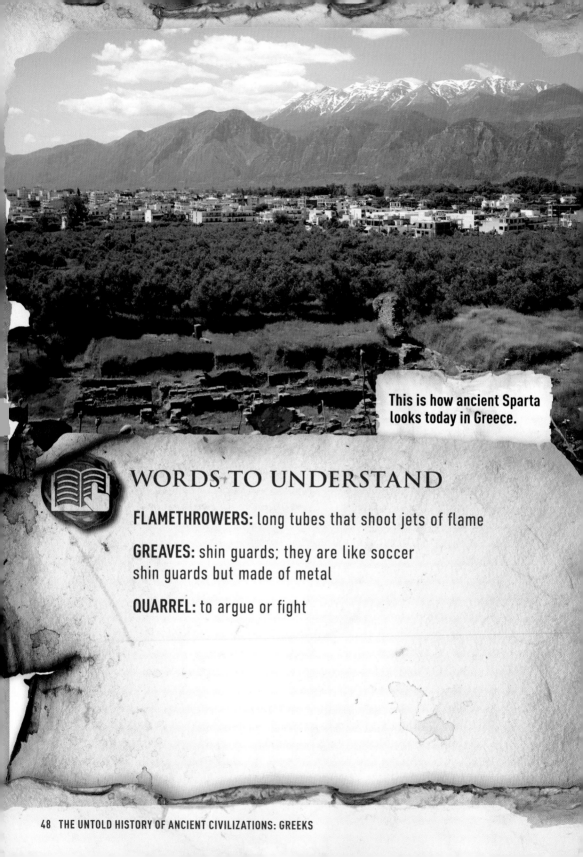

This is how ancient Sparta looks today in Greece.

WORDS TO UNDERSTAND

FLAMETHROWERS: long tubes that shoot jets of flame

GREAVES: shin guards; they are like soccer shin guards but made of metal

QUARREL: to argue or fight

CHAPTER 10

WAR INSIDE AND OUT

The Greeks were fierce warriors. And, unfortunately, they usually fought among themselves. Rival city-states **quarreled** over land and trade. Athens and Sparta were some of the most powerful rivals. Great cities were destroyed, and many brave men died. Twice, the Greeks united, more or less, to defeat an outside enemy, the Persians. They also fought against the Turkish city of Troy.

Most wars were short. Fighting stopped in late summer because soldiers had to help with harvesting. It stopped in winter, too, because the weather was bad. Only Sparta stayed ready to fight all year round. Unlike other Greeks, the Spartan culture revolved around the military. Spartan soldiers wore uniforms and marched to army bands. The noise of Spartan flute players could be deafening. Mothers in Sparta wanted their

HOW TO WIN A WAR

The Greeks invented fearsome war machines, such as giant crossbows armed with iron-tipped arrows and huge catapults, called ballistas, that hurled lumps of rock at enemy walls. They even made **flamethrowers**. To fight against attacks from the sea, Archimedes built the claw of Archimedes, which actually lifted and tipped ships coming in to shore. But many Greek soldiers preferred traditional tactics in war. They destroyed crops and cut down olive trees, so everyone starved. They surrounded cities until food and water ran out or the citizens all died of disease.

This ancient medieval catapult is designed after the ancient Greek ballistas.

Leonidas was king of Sparta.

sons to be brave. Before a battle, they told them, "Come back carrying your shield or on it (dead!)."

All men in Sparta became professional soldiers, but poor men had a hard time affording the equipment. Each Greek hoplite (infantryman) had to buy his own shield, helmet, breastplate, spear, sword, and **greaves** (shin guards). Poor men had to make do with cheap weapons like slingshots and had no protection from enemy attack.

TEXT-DEPENDENT QUESTIONS

1. Who were the biggest rivals in ancient Greece?
2. What were some of the war machines created by the Greeks?
3. When did most wars stop? Why?

RESEARCH PROJECT

MAKE A GREEK SHIELD

Each Greek hoplite (soldier) carried his own large wooden shield. You can make your own using paper plates or cardboard!

You will need:

- Cardboard
- A pencil or pen
- Paint or colored markers
- Glue

Directions:

First, draw a large circle on a piece of cardboard. The easiest method is to find a large container to trace. Cut out the circle. Decorate your shield by painting or coloring your design. You can do an Internet search for Greek shield designs to help you decide how to decorate it. Finally, you will need two holders in the back of the shield. Cut out two strips of cardboard or paper that will fit around your arm. Glue those two strips to the back of the shield so that you can place your arm through the holders. This will keep your shield secure.

Adapted from Activity Village.co.uk

Not every ancient Greek man could afford a soldier's gear such as what's seen on this statue of a hoplite.

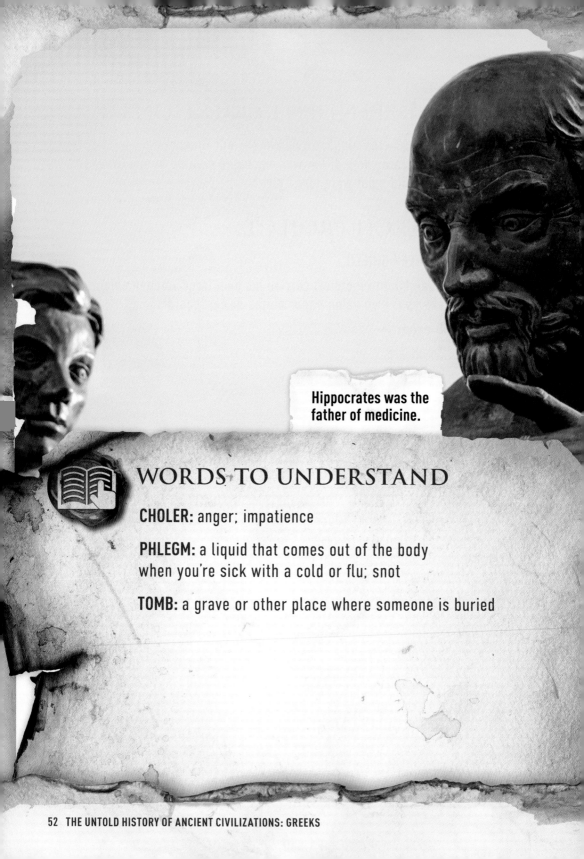

Hippocrates was the father of medicine.

WORDS TO UNDERSTAND

CHOLER: anger; impatience

PHLEGM: a liquid that comes out of the body when you're sick with a cold or flu; snot

TOMB: a grave or other place where someone is buried

CHAPTER 11

THIS LIFE AND THE NEXT

The Greeks attacked disease with magic, medicine, religion, and sometimes science. But still, their life spans were short. The average Greek woman lived until she was thirty-five. (Childbirth was very dangerous.) A man might live longer, maybe until fifty. Many children died before they were five years old.

Greek doctors thought that people had four different liquids, called humors, flowing through their bodies—red blood, green **phlegm**, yellow bile, and black **choler**. Disease began when the humors were out of balance. Doctors tested (and tasted!) samples to diagnose illnesses.

The people of ancient Greece believed that Asclepius, the god of medicine and healing, could help heal them.

One famous doctor had different ideas. His name was Hippocrates (about 460–370 BC), and he became the father of medicine. He studied his patients scientifically. He believed that illness was caused by an unhealthy lifestyle or an unquiet mind. He also said doctors should be clean, neat, slim, sweet smelling, and good looking! Patients would trust them more that way.

RIDDLE ME THIS

Greek legends describe a terrifying monster called the Sphinx. It lay in wait for travelers. When you came along, you had to answer this riddle: "What has four legs, then two, then three?" The answer is "a human" (a baby crawls on four legs, an adult walks on two legs, and an old person walks with a stick). If you didn't know the answer, the Sphinx would eat you.

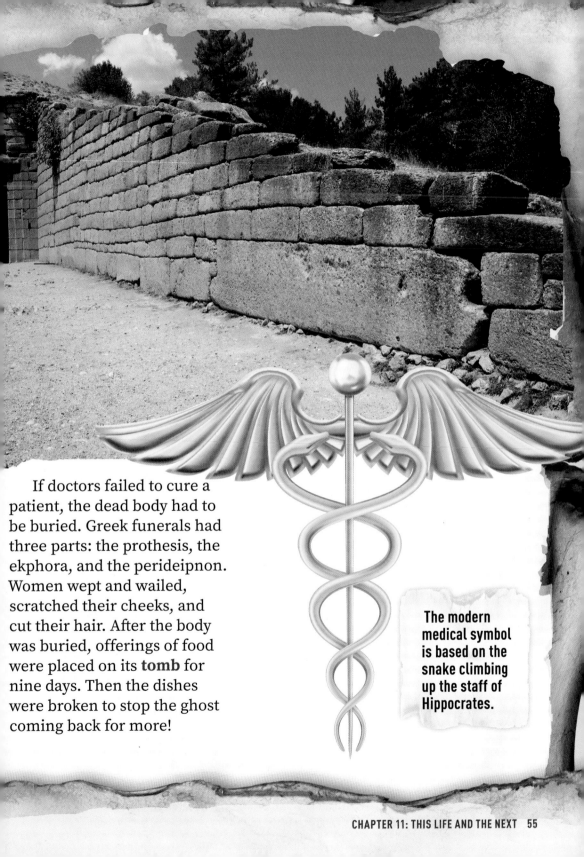

If doctors failed to cure a patient, the dead body had to be buried. Greek funerals had three parts: the prothesis, the ekphora, and the perideipnon. Women wept and wailed, scratched their cheeks, and cut their hair. After the body was buried, offerings of food were placed on its **tomb** for nine days. Then the dishes were broken to stop the ghost coming back for more!

The modern medical symbol is based on the snake climbing up the staff of Hippocrates.

This ancient Greece scene found on pottery consists of a Centaur, people, and gods of Olympus.

This video can help you paint using the Greek method.

TEXT-DEPENDENT QUESTIONS

1. Why did Greek women typically have a shorter life span than men?
2. Who was considered "the father of medicine"?
3. What happened to the dishes left on top of the tomb?

RESEARCH PROJECT

PAINT BACK-TO-FRONT, GREEK-STYLE

You will need:

- Colored paper
- A pen or pencil
- Black paint
- Paint brush

Follow steps 1 to 3 below to see if you can paint back-to-front in the Greek way.

Directions:

Greek craft workers liked to decorate the pots they made with scenes from everyday life or with pictures of gods and heroes. Often, they used a special back-to-front technique.

1. They drew the outline of the gods or people they wanted to show.
2. They painted the background black, leaving the rest unpainted.
3. Sometimes they added details, like eyes or hair, to the unpainted area.

This ancient Greek vase displays the back-to-front technique and shows daily activities.

GREEK FACTS

The Karyatides statues, Erehtheio, on the Acropolis in Athens, Greece.

MEN ONLY: Women were banned at the Olympic Games. But one mother was so keen to see her son race that she dressed as a man and hid among the crowd. When she saw her son winning, she shouted out with excitement and gave herself away. She was expelled in disgrace.

TRICKSTER: Athenian ruler Peisistratus (about 600–527 BC) seized power with a clever trick. He rushed into town one day, covered in mud and bruises, claiming to have been attacked. He asked the citizens' assembly to give him a bodyguard, and they agreed. He used this bodyguard to defeat his enemies and take control of the city.

A bust of Archimedes.

SMELLY FEET: Priests at the temple of Zeus at Dodona, southern Greece, were known as selloi, which means "with unwashed feet." No one knows why they were so dirty!

MARATHON MAN: In ancient Greece, urgent wartime messages were carried by fast runners. The most famous was called Pheidippides. It was said that he ran 26 miles (42 km) from a battlefield at Marathon in 490 BC to tell the Athenians that their army had won. He then dropped dead from exhaustion!

LUCKY FOR SOME: For the Greeks, right was lucky, and left was unlucky. When the Greek general Xenophon (about 435–354 BC) was preparing for battle in 401 BC, he heard an eagle screeching on his right-hand side. Priests told him this meant he would win. He did.

THE WORLD'S GREATEST WARRIOR? Most Greeks thought Alexander the Great (356–323 BC) was the greatest soldier who ever lived. Some said he was a god. Alexander became king of Macedonia (north of Greece) when he was only twenty years old. He murdered his younger brother to make sure he never became king. Then he set off to conquer the world. He built a vast empire, stretching from Greece and Egypt to India and Afghanistan. He wanted more, but his army refused to march farther. He died at age thirty-two in Iraq.

THE ANCIENT GREEKS VISITED BRITAIN: Explorer Pytheas reached Orkney and Shetland around 350 BC. The Greeks also sailed along the coast of Africa and may have crossed the equator.

I'VE GOT IT! Greek mathematician and inventor Archimedes (287–212 BC) was one of the greatest scientists of all time. After he discovered how pulleys and levers work, he boasted, "Give me somewhere to stand, and I will move the Earth!" He also became famous for making a very important discovery (about mass and gravity) in his bath. He was so excited that he jumped out and ran down the street, shouting "Eureka!" (I've got it!).

A bronze relief of Alexander the Great riding a chariot.

FURTHER RESOURCES

FURTHER READING

Burgan, Michael. *Ancient Greeks*. Chicago, IL: Word Book, 2009.

Catel, Patrick. *What Did the Ancient Greeks Do for Me?* Chicago, IL. Heinemann Library, 2011.

Green, Jen. *Hail! Ancient Greeks*. New York: Crabtree Pubs., 2011.

Miles, Liz. *Meet the Ancient Greeks*. New York: Gareth Stevens Publishing, 2015.

Schomp, Virginia. *The Ancient Greeks*. New York: Marshall Cavendish Benchmark, 2008.

Many ancient Greek homes had only one entrance that was kept guarded for security.

INTERNET RESOURCES

The Internet is a great way to find out more about the Greeks. But the Internet is changing constantly, so if you can't find these websites, try searching using the words "ancient Greeks."

Ancient Greece for Kids
http://www.historyforkids.org/
    learn/greeks/index.htm

The Ancient Greek World
http://www.penn.museum/
    sites/greek_world/

The Ancient Olympics
http://www.perseus.tufts.edu/Olympics

Aesop's Fables
http://www.aesopfables.com/

**National Geographic for Kids—Tales
    of Terror from Ancient Greece**
http://www.ngkids.co.uk/
    history/Greek-Myths

This monument of Diogenes in Turkey features the barrel he lived in and a statue of him and his dog.

EDUCATIONAL VIDEO LINKS

Greeks1: Watch this video for a brief history of Ancient Greece. http://x-qr.net/1EWE

Greeks2: This video explains how women were viewed in different city-states in ancient Greece. http://x-qr.net/1D05

Greeks3: This school project by Madeline Webb demonstrates the different clothing styles for men and women of ancient Greece.   http://x-qr.net/1HKU

Greeks4: This video can help you paint using the Greek method. http://x-qr.net/1FQF

PHOTO CREDITS

Cover: © Alberto Loyo | Shutterstock, © Kokhanchikov | Shutterstock; Front Matter: © Cardaf | Shutterstock;; Chapter 1: © Nice_Media_PRODUCTION | Shutterstock, © uladzimir zgurski | Shutterstock, © Marzolino | Shutterstock, © DinoPh | Shutterstock; Chapter 2: © Feel good studio | Shutterstock, © Almotional | Shutterstock, © Shelli Jensen | Shutterstock, © Anna_Pustynnikova | Shutterstock; Chapter 3: © Anastasios71 | Shutterstock, © DreamArt123 |Shutterstock, © Vladimir Zhoga | Shutterstock; Chapter 4: © Sergey Goryachev | Shutterstock, © Alexandros Michailidis | Shutterstock, © Vladimir Korostyshevskiy | Shutterstock, © TeodorLazarev | Shutterstock, © Anastasios71 | Shutterstock; Chapter 5: © Robert Kneschke| Shutterstock, © Photo Oz | Shutterstock, © Anton_Ivanov | Shutterstock , © Alexandros Michailidis | Shutterstock, © Cicero Castro | Shutterstock; Chapter 6: © Jarek Pajewski | Shutterstock, © shaifulzamri | Shutterstock, © yasuhiro amano | Shutterstock, © mountainpix | Shutterstock; Chapter 7: © Masson | Shutterstock, © Gilmanshin | Shutterstock; Chapter 8: © Nice_Media_PRODUCTION | Shutterstock, © Aerial-motion | Shutterstock, © aleksandr4300 | Shutterstock, © f8grapher | Shutterstock; Chapter 9: © BlackMac | Shutterstock, © anyaivanova | Shutterstock, © IMG Stock Studio | Shutterstock, © Samot | Shutterstock; Chapter 10: © Taneli Karjalainen | Shutterstock, © Luxerendering | Shutterstock, © Anastasios71 | Shutterstock, © Cromagnon | Shutterstock; Chapter 11: © Michail Patakos |Shutterstock , © Lefteris Papaulakis | Shutterstock, © Violeta Meleti | Shutterstock, © Natykach Nataliia | Shutterstock, © matrioshka | Shutterstock, © Kamira | Shutterstock; Back Matter: © Georgios Tsichlis | Shutterstock, © claudio zaccherini | Shutterstock, © Cromagnon | Shutterstock, © Djsash | Shutterstock, © GEORGE STAMATIS | Shutterstock

INDEX

Gypsum Public Library
P.O. Box 979 / 47 Lundgren Blvd.
Gypsum, CO 81637
(970) 524-5080